Community Helpers
Dentists

by Cari Meister

Bullfrog Books

Ideas for Parents and Teachers

Bullfrog Books let children practice reading informational text at the earliest reading levels. Repetition, familiar words, and photo labels support early readers.

Before Reading

- Discuss the cover photo. What does it tell them?
- Look at the picture glossary together. Read and discuss the words.

Read the Book

- "Walk" through the book and look at the photos. Let the child ask questions. Point out the photo labels.
- Read the book to the child, or have him or her read independently.

After Reading

- Prompt the child to think more. Ask: Have you been to the dentist? What work did the dentist do for your teeth?

Bullfrog Books are published by Jump!
5357 Penn Avenue South
Minneapolis, MN 55419
www.jumplibrary.com

Library of Congress Cataloging-in-Publication Data
Meister, Cari.
  Dentists / by Cari Meister.
    pages cm. —(Community helpers)
  Summary: "This photo-illustrated book for early readers tells what dentists do and how they work to keep our teeth healthy" —Provided by publisher.
  Includes bibliographical references and index.
  ISBN 978-1-62031-091-5 (hardcover)
  ISBN 978-1-62496-159-5 (ebook)
  ISBN 978-1-62031-135-6 (paperback)
  1. Dentistry —Juvenile literature.
  2. Dentists —Juvenile literature.
  3. Teeth —Care and hygiene —Juvenile literature.
  I. Title.
  RK63.M45 2015
  617.6'0232 —dc23
                    2013039885

Editor: Wendy Dieker
Series Designer: Ellen Huber
Book Designer: Lindaanne Donohoe
Photo Researcher: Kurtis Kinneman

Photo Credits: All photos by Shutterstock except Alamy, 12-13, 18; Dreamstime cover, 10, 18-19, 22, 23bl; Superstock 14-15, 23tr; iStock 21

Printed in the United States of America at Corporate Graphics, North Mankato, Minnesota.
6-2014
10 9 8 7 6 5 4 3 2 1

Table of Contents

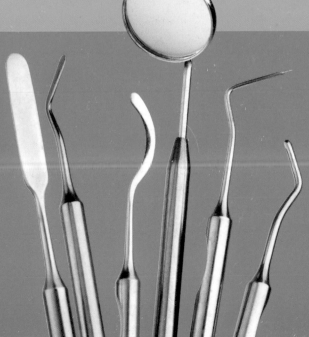

Dentists at Work

Ben wants to be a dentist.

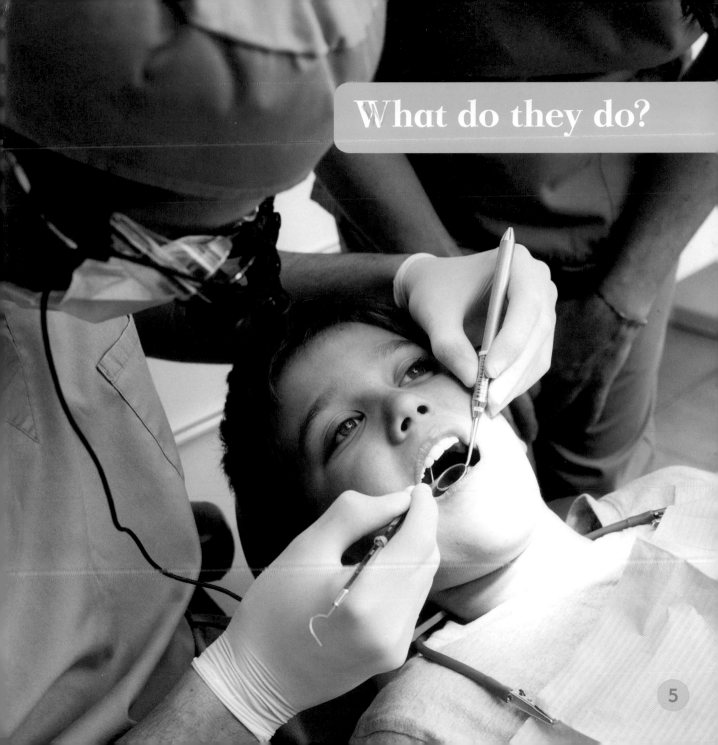

What do they do?

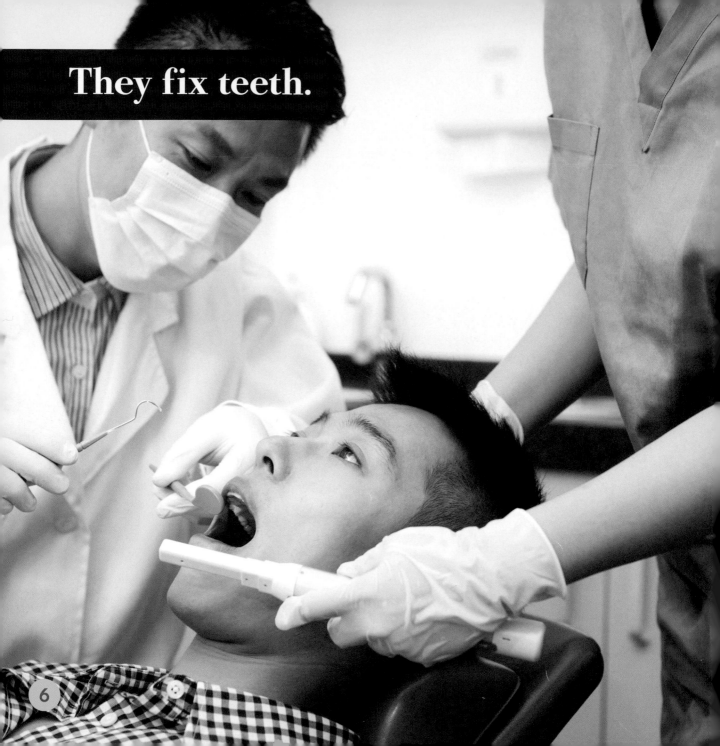

They fix teeth.

They help keep teeth healthy.

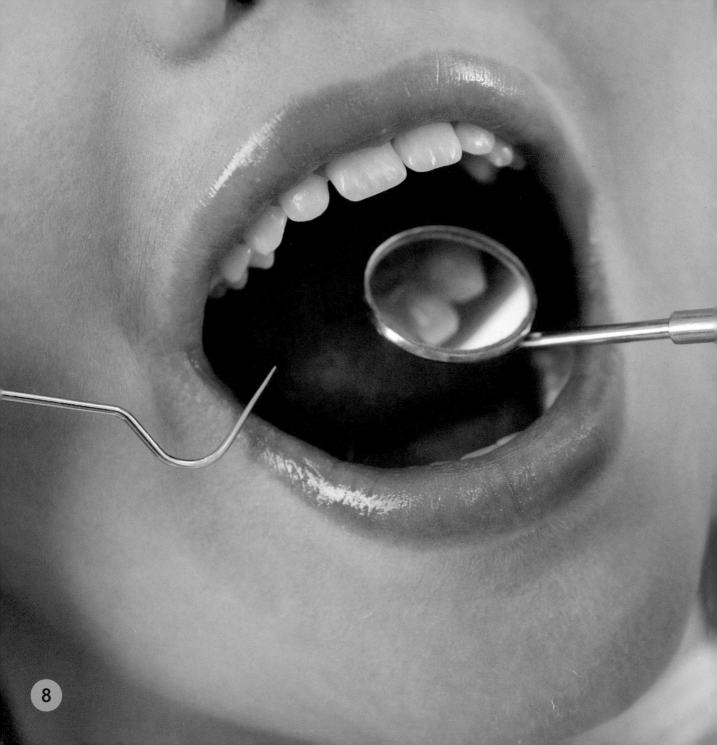

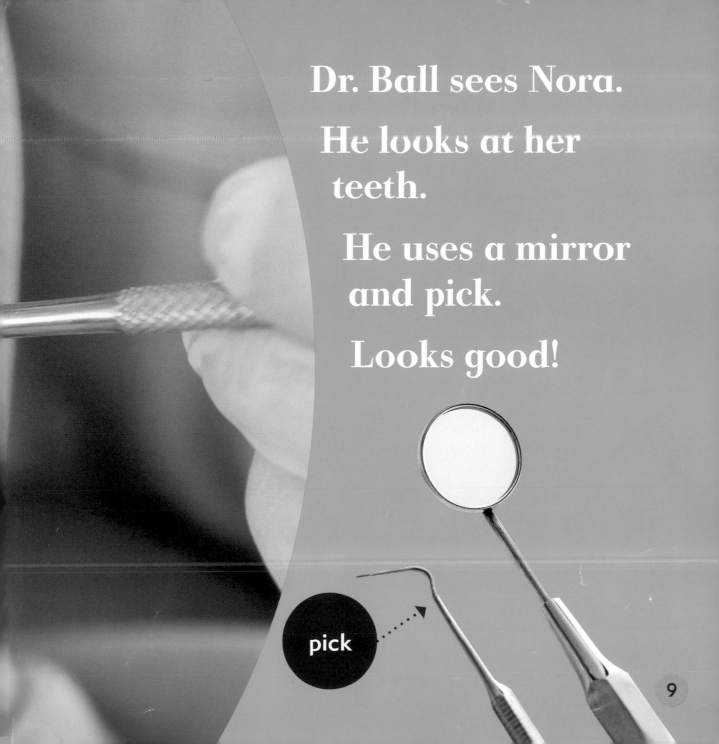

Dr. Ball sees Nora.

He looks at her teeth.

He uses a mirror and pick.

Looks good!

pick

Dot helps the dentist.

She cleans Mia's teeth.

Open up!

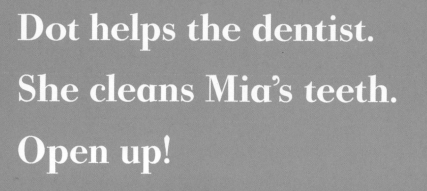

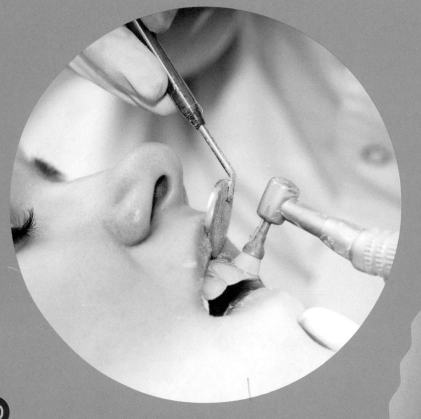

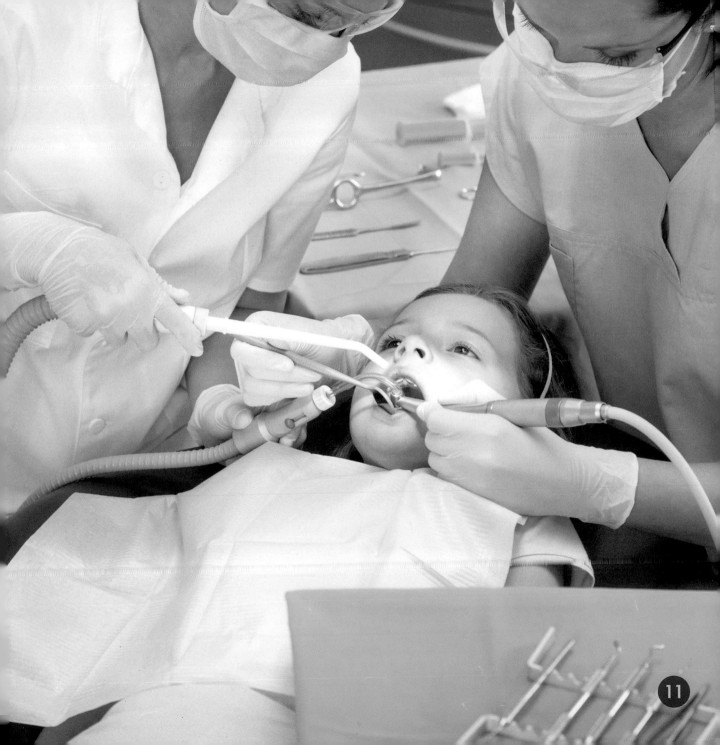

Dr. Vu takes an x-ray.

Look at the picture.

You can see under the gums.

Wow!

x-ray

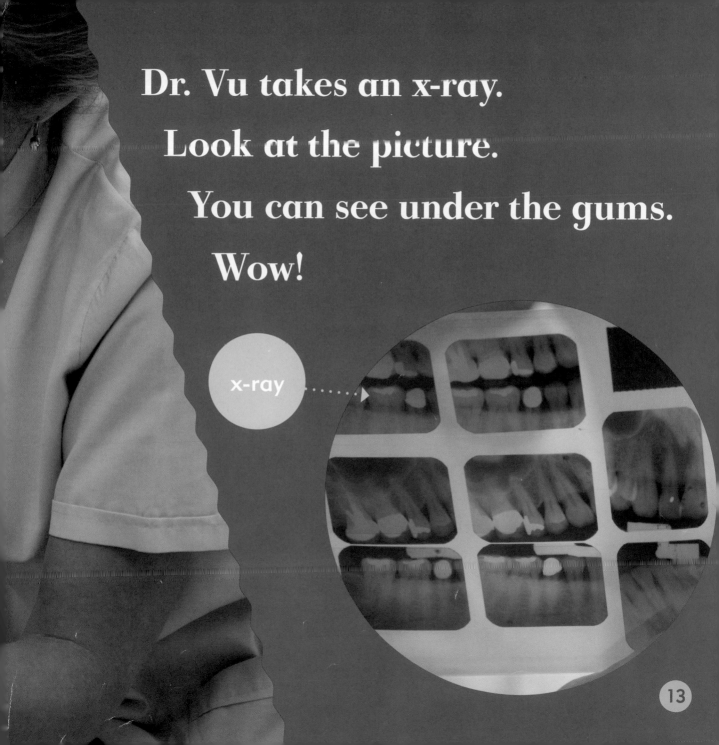

Dr. West shows Ava
how to use floss.

It cleans in
between teeth.

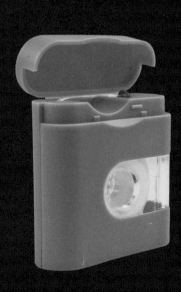

floss

Oh no!

Tod's tooth hurts.

16

cavity

It has a hole.

It is a cavity.

Dr. Lee can fix it.

He puts in a filling.

All better!

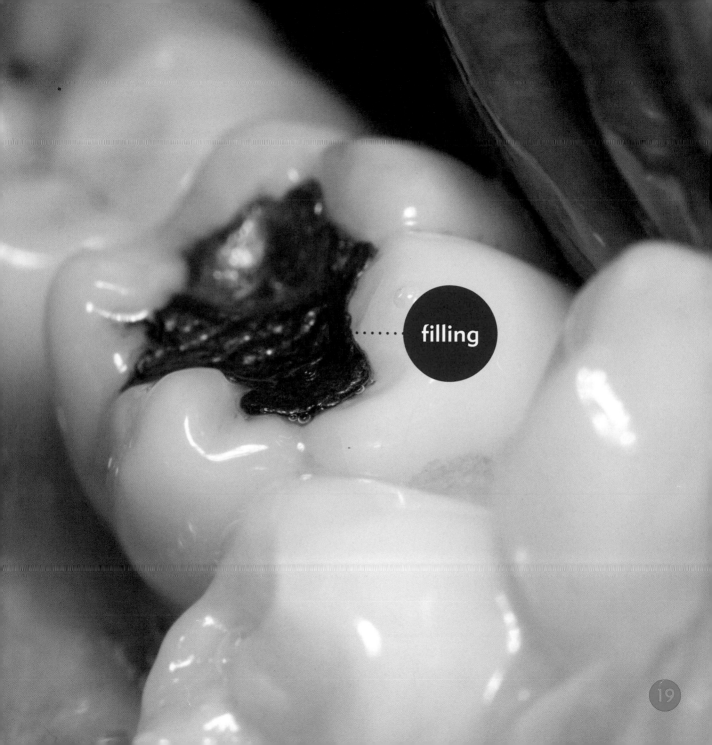

filling

Dentists do good work!

At the Dentist's Office

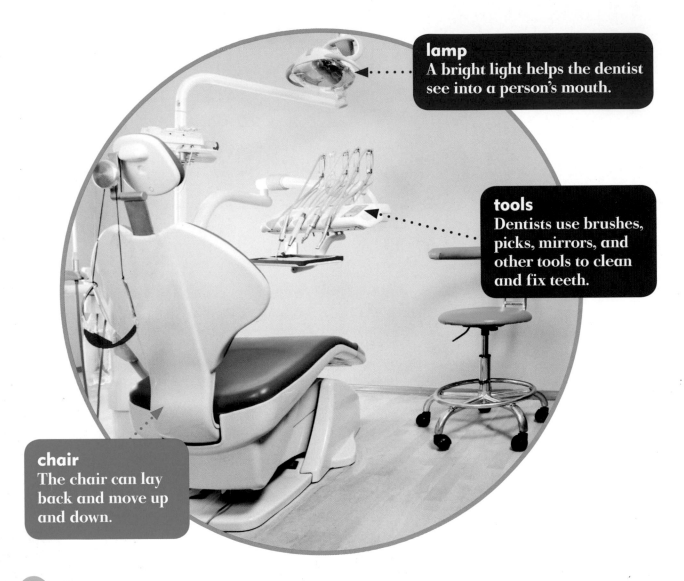

lamp
A bright light helps the dentist see into a person's mouth.

tools
Dentists use brushes, picks, mirrors, and other tools to clean and fix teeth.

chair
The chair can lay back and move up and down.

Picture Glossary

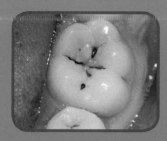

cavity
A small hole in a tooth.

floss
A thin string pulled between the teeth to clean them.

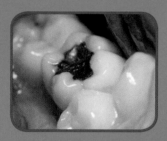

filling
Something (like cement or gold) used to fill a hole in a tooth.

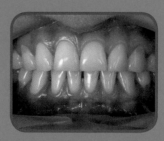

gums
The pink skin around the base of the teeth.

Index

To Learn More

Learning more is as easy as 1, 2, 3.

1) Go to www.factsurfer.com

2) Enter "dentists" into the search box.

3) Click the "Surf" button to see a list of websites.

With factsurfer.com, finding more information is just a click away.